Candy Floss

Candy Floss

Bhavyakirti

Published by
Rupa Publications India Pvt. Ltd 2022
7/16, Ansari Road, Daryaganj
New Delhi 110002

Sales centres:
Allahabad Bengaluru Chennai
Hyderabad Jaipur Kathmandu
Kolkata Mumbai

Copyright © Bhavyakirti 2022
Illustrations: Amith Das

This is a work of fiction. Names, characters, places and incidents are either the product of the author's imagination or are used fictitiously and any resemblance to any actual person, living or dead, events or locales is entirely coincidental.

All rights reserved.

No part of this publication may be reproduced, transmitted, or stored in a retrieval system, in any form or by any means, electronic, mechanical, photocopying, recording or otherwise, without the prior permission of the publisher.

ISBN: 978-93-5520-076-1

Fourth impression 2022

10 9 8 7 6 5 4

Printed in India

This book is sold subject to the condition that it shall not, by way of trade or otherwise, be lent, resold, hired out, or otherwise circulated, without the publisher's prior consent, in any form of binding or cover other than that in which it is published.

Contents

In Today's News	1
Market Walls and Railings	3
Hydrochloride and Other Bathroom Essentials	5
Degrees Are À La Carte	6
The Bookstore Outside Which No One Wishes to Stand	9
Stories from My Kitchen	11
Canvases Are Sad Because We Paint on Anything Now	13
Conversations	15
Unfinished Idea	17
Binary Fission	19
Of Buffets	21
Detergent	23
Higher Education	25
Candy Floss	27
Drinking Cold Brew Out of a Hot Coffee Pot	28
Homes	29

Days and Nights Make Days	31
Inspired by Nissim Ezekiel	32
Glass Bangles	34
Sports Injuries	37
At Night I Think of Ability	39
Aerodynamics	41
What if I Met You at My Favourite Restaurant?	43
We Buried Her in Compost	45
Summers With You	47
Prelude to 'This Is Just to Say'	48
Painting Skin on Skin	49
Full Moons	51
In Memoriam	52
I Stopped Seeing People Again Today	57
Rails Are Midnight to Me	58
Empty Hand Cream	59
Seating Them on Park Benches	61
Mumbai	62
Birth	63

Quantum	64
What Will You Do?	65
Fish Tank	66
Summer Love	67
Qualifications I Don't Have to Write My First Book	68

In Today's News

I.

Mother seated front-right, commanding traffic
from inside her white sedan; I, strapped in
the back seat, paper-weighted with bare texts
of highlighted legislations.

In place of the radio tattled I, stuttering the
numbers on the far left, and thereafter the
marked text. Zigzagging through a
metal maze, jumping red lights—

Halting before a studio in the sandy brick
of home. They saved business tax, we
saved a higher fee on peewee art class
in safe, gated colonies.

II.

Vermilion return my sheets and I.
Hands scrubbed under elusive sinks. She
tells me I am two apples and a nose, my
cheeks glow like Kashmir apples—

a lacerated sun, slathered
across the stem of growing fruits. I thought
of marmalade then, seen only in pictures,
most jams were dandelion yellow

except ours. We spread only red. But *she* looked
like apricots, her burgeoning motherhood
seven years fresh, dimpled the skin. I
saw apricots, the hint of a wrinkle, her face

smooth and yellow.

III.

I am in today's news, in sight, in flight
behind a suited woman—a glance of me, where
she streams her news. I tell my mother they were
interviewing old businesses closing.

Red shirts suit young women better, yellow
dulls the eyes, the jaundiced face of the
crowd, of the background noise. I hear her,
I drop the line, she'll forget about it if

I am home in time.

Market Walls and Railings

Who do you wait around for
half-empty paper cup of tea?

Your skin peeled,
stuck to the sides,
hatred forgotten,
you were loathed,
now you lay harmless,
friendless.

Slabs punctuate the railing against which
stood your people yester-night, mornings
disperse them like sunlight,
like the bubbles of your nascent broil.

Hydrochloride and Other Bathroom Essentials

Fatigue caressed at night
and the mornings don't care
much for sunlight.
The rubber-elastic of the days
twangs sharp by five.

The malleable watch-hand
my hand-watch, or wrist hangs
around my bluing finger
it knows time, or stopped knowing
when I stopped looking, I wouldn't know.

Maybe the watch-hands
have slithered out like baby
snakes that slink away from
the rusted bathroom sink like
there may be no
       tomorrow.

My bottle of hydrochloride will tell you there isn't.

Degrees Are À La Carte

I.

It is windy today. Ladies flock to my report card.
Take it. Take it. Health. Pamphlets fly in the wind,
You too are destined to.

II.

My cheque is heavy. I wave
my water-crinkled fingers
in biting-cold air. Outside,
an Ambassador waits for me.
I had seen it in a photograph.
Titled? 1960. Some family's.

I know, I know. The blue
of my cape silks the day.
Every other more than the next.
New, now. Next. Novel.
New-fangled. *How many more
words did you learn?* Many,
comparatively.

I write avant-garde.
I left behind the five lined.

My mother prides.
Now she italicizes words.
How else should one decide where
to sit? I think of the ladies
sometimes, still flocking maybe.

Or maybe they are replete;
striking words, circling words,
Adding words in between
sentence spaces; selling more,
More, many receipts.

Bhavyakirti

The Bookstore Outside Which No One Wishes to Stand

I.

I held hands with the book in the store, as had
                you the day before, our fingers entwined atop

the black of words. Your lingering touch sickled
                the edges, the bend-back was a lazy chore.

II.

Do not touch if you wish not to purchase
                we sell gloved favourites, and only the chaste.

Like the birds that drop eggs post a caress,
                our patrons prefer the virtuous to embrace.

Bhavyakirti

Stories from My Kitchen

Evening shelves
trouble—trepidation
of wet dishes—the
persistent humidity—
my wet arms
placing semi-wiped
dishwasher unsafe
crockery on metal ledges.
Water stained ledges
reveal to me that

it is the cliffs
that push, as can they.
Why does the floor call
the most delicate water
glasses? Easy prey.
At night I think about
the most wonderful
lives led by ordinary
people. I think about
their kitchens. I think
about

the spoons they do
not hate—their shelves
dripping anything but

vengeance—the echo
of champagne clinks
across their tables—
the
whir
of automated
dishwashers that ask
nothing of them.

Today if I hang kitchen
decorations, it would be
home magazine covers.
The more one sees, the more
one knows. My thin spoons
will learn not to bend,
maybe. Maybe my shelves
will whimper in
Replaceable font.

Canvases Are Sad Because We Paint on Anything Now

An artist's canvases are upset,
gathering dust under glory garnering
painted vases, and murals moved
from walls to faces,

acrylic dabbed on compact discs and
under mugs on coasters, on extinct TV
screens and digitally created posters.
Hidden floor tiles are also,
printed.

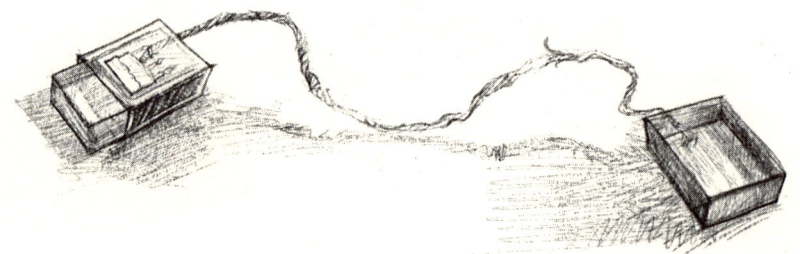

Bhavyakirti

Conversations

Learn something about my personal fiancé, I mean finance. When you sit in my living room, ramble about your greens; I will about mine.

Who has it worse? We shall compete. My stereo will play the distant chiding
of our parents' money-talks, the ruffle of note-whips in stale bedrooms.

Iron out smaller denominations with me, lament at our marriages to
worldly affairs. Race the roll of coins, the toss of die, the gamble of

raindrops clinging to beat car windows. Later when you egress, I will
rejoice at your plight. My Doritos are a swindler's worth, if luck be

my lady tonight. The hundred I gave you for a cab will double in
tomorrow's lunch of debt. Investments count on pride and shame,

and tears in a tête-à-tête.

Bhavyakirti

Unfinished Idea

Someone smells constantly like wet laundry.

Hair escapes from the loose elastic strung up
high on her head
but nothing else at all escapes from her arms.

The bags slung across her shoulders
aren't weight as you think, she
unloads the troubles of her day
into a clean sink.

The bowl of fruit is inhumanly polished,
bright glints or beams or strokes
of yellow, white light drawn from end to end
of the dining hall.

Nothing at all escapes from her hands, they
bind tight like black rubber bands.

Bhavyakirti

Binary Fission

I had left two cups on the kitchen slab,
one stained with the yellow sugar of a tangy
lemon, one so fresh and white I could hide
it on my sheets.

My mother stood horrified, paralyzed
in fear before the crime scene I had created.
What were wars and modern plague when
chaos and order stood together at her door

and she could fend for herself and me
with only a plastic sieve? I swore I had no
memory of why I released havoc
but she wouldn't hear it.

My mother stood with a cup in each
hand, and wondered whether to turn
right to the sink or left to the shelf.
I thought I should gracefully ease her

task and lend her a hand but she
probably wouldn't know which one to
free up. She still stands there today, I am
growing old and she is splitting.

Bhavyakirti

Of Buffets

Of buffets; the plain illusion of choice,
of range, of disease, in webs of sugar detected
loud under stethoscopes; of stable society,
of lavish weddings, of continental breakfasts.

Of buffets; the overt manifestation
of false free will, of offers most detested
of the choice of choice over the identification
of fancies.

Bhavyakirti

Detergent

Blue powder foams white, clouds

my clothes silk, strained, squeezed
then stiff, wanting the opacity of
hard water.

Blue power scratches and melts

across my white sink, stuck on loofahs
like icing on a hot day
in black piping bags.

Blue powder crusts on the

underside of forearms, cunningly
hidden away from the scourge
of increased tap flow and tissues.

Blue powder spills on laundry

dishes, mocks the wet hands that
seek to pick it up, spills, spills
in boxes, on floors, in book spines
after innocent page turns.

Bhavyakirti

Higher Education

An hour before midnight we sat across each
other, bowing heads to farcical choices,
water in our shared plastic bottle rippled
with page turns and environmental guilt.

An hour after midnight we walked
around unholy fields, spinning our keys in
our fingers and denting the bottle in a
glissando across the trees.

At 3 a.m., we sat across each other
yet again, cross-legged on a sandstone bench,
hiding from crunches in the gravel and
wishing to dissolve into the night, then
we threw the bottle away.

At 8 a.m., you knocked at my door and
asked me for my pitcher, I looked
at the crescents under your eyes and readied
you for fresh dispiriting of fresher days.

Bhavyakirti

Candy Floss

Smoke-blue and pink clouds
wrapped around a cane
as long as the panorama of
pastel maternity wards.

Pulled over the dirty gloss of
thrice-folded brochures in stacks.
Fluff dissolves and sticks unto
hands, morphine fades away

and empty hallways echo with
the prying of plastic from plastic.
Everywhere we celebrate the
original utilitarian, everywhere

we don't.

Drinking Cold Brew Out of a Hot Coffee Pot

Effective remain magic porridge pots
not hot pots cradled on rickety tables—

they stick; catalyzed into an old marriage
by old coffee-spills and sugar slips.

Staffers glance in sympathy or with
sad smirks, or in detestable nods

as they queue behind the grand, old man,
the coffee pot of meetings past.

Homes

My city is glass panels and
fresh buildings and a few metro stations away
from 1100 to the present.

Common hot iron'd,
sharp-edged knives slice away life from life
my city doesn't know who the outliers are.

Rattling windows will not tell
if the wind ruffles the trees or it is the slow build up
of the whistles of blackened pressure cookers

that escape framed, wooden meshes somewhat
along the smoky fumes of mosquito repellent coils
or lethally-sweetened scent machines

depending on where you stand.
Gutters might stink of human waste or your
gutters might stink of human waste that
you can't smell.

Bhavyakirti

Days and Nights Make Days

I picked at unripe scabs to expose
the fresh, pink skin to the wrath of day.

I rot away and chip into the night
as do other nocturnal insects.

Inspired by Nissim Ezekiel

I.

Father's getting old.
I never did notice until now
when he closed his eyes to rest
and I looked upon his face
to see his salt-and-pepper hair
shining in the brightness
of the tube light in his office.

Just about to reach the mid-length
of his life, he seems to be
taking on the antics of age
mumbling about the colour of my socks,
my short hours at the study desk,
the unorganised stack of papers
lying in my room.

II.

Father's getting old.
I can see him fret more often
creases on his face like that
of the papers in his office
his mouth turned upside down

into a frown, and worry
evident from the ridges
on his forehead.

Sitting at the computer for long hours
he hears the sound of his phone ringtone
to which he's slowly becoming immune;
when he lays to rest with nothing
in his hands
I can make out it is because he
has too much on his mind.

III.

Father's getting old.
Sometimes he laughs mindlessly
at banters between his children
that remind him of himself at their age

he cries when he hears of an uncle dying,
steeped in memories four decades old
he coughs, and plays with his fingers.

Thoughts swirl in his head faster
than the milk does in his tea.

Glass Bangles

I. The long and winded

Look at her bangles, gleaming in tinkles of victory
on summer afternoons. The ripple of those cascading
on dressing drawers in a huff of baby powder on sweat-filmed
wrists. She carefully dusts the bed now, the ghost
of her harlequin glass percussions like a phantom limb.
You wouldn't miss it in the corner of a school jazz band.
When she dunks her head into the morning bucket,
her warm, slow breath melts into the chilly water, you
wouldn't see bubbles, you'd see a current, like the butter
dissolving by the sides of her saucer, unlike the staccato of
her finger that measures its temperature.

II. The short and quick

Today is for estimates.
She wheels in approximates of pulses,
wheat and rice, shopping
carts are dull before her,
the essentials torrent into bags, then
boxes, then pans, then plates.
Her palm blisters under the weight
of hot dishes. Her trays lie
in unproductive agony. The red of

her arms taunts accountability.
She remembers freezing dead
in the middle of a busy road.

Yesteryear it was the stupor
of self-running wheels.
Today, her eyes crinkle in embarrassment,
the heat of the old stove
cracks her glass bangles.

Here ends the matter.

Sports Injuries

Ice-cold coals peel skin
denaturing under water.
The nurse corkscrews her
fingers with gauze.

Why don't you—
peel off layers
of skin,
display those before me? And
those before them?

    Display?

    display depth,
    display lucidity,
    display precision.

Agility in sport is reward, what of? Of
mornings. What about the morning feels so
final? Is it the drying dew? The dying moon?
Athletes and others down

lukewarm water from warm Nike bottles arranged
in rainbows on summer afternoons. Taste plastic,

health betadine dripping

Candy Floss

from forehead to the corner of the lip, dark like liquid coal.
Tongues charred in white, other things, skin-clinging

onto-TV-characters-stamped-across-t-shirts. No,
sorry, printed
jersey numbers.

At Night I Think of Ability

I think of my hand limp at the side of my mattress, of my fingers
carved like a sceptre had gently slipped from my oily grip. Did they
see this when they sculpted deadened arms? When you look next
at a white statue, look carefully for my sunk nails, the cuticles creeping
on keratin, the sharp dent on my knuckles where flesh tears to discharge
nail, bone shies from epidermis, veins split into rivulets snake
around the unusual, veins pumped with liquid ceramic dry out slowly.

When you knock at me carefully, you'll hear the echo of a chamber
lined doubly; the inside untouched by sandpaper—rough and ridged;
the outside is not amenable to the tips of your fingers, not to your finger-
prints, not to your fingers dressed down under cloth.

Bhavyakirti

Aerodynamics

How does she fly her paper planes that way?
Her folds and creases crassly done,
her precision landing like flies on skin,
her Wikihow prints fanned from the corner staple,
her Wikihow prints lie upturned, look—
that's discarded information.
She plays by ear,
her thumbprints mark door handles around her house,
her thumbs smudge the ink of trebles and clefs on door handles.
Why else is there music in her step?
How does she fly paper planes that way?
Lines run across the underside of her planes.
Do you understand?
It isn't the force of wind.
Some music plays in some room where you don't stand.
You search the tabs on your computer—
where does it come from?
Her paper planes still fly.
Her papers tear from staples and autumn the tiles.
Her paper planes still fly.
Can you find the music?

What if I Met You at My Favourite Restaurant?

I found you seated on a sofa
              in a dim lit restaurant, jewelled
as a crown somewhere in the
              middle of a busy street. At
restaurants, I avoided (hard-backed)
              seats—today is assessment—
velvet couches whisper that faux leather
              hides mesh and unidentifiable brown

cloth under. The faux leather complains
              of armchairs canoodling embroidered
cushions. Your elbow impression rises
              and falls, ventilating in rhythm with
the mobile device of
              your darkest habits. Today I am
in awe of your nonchalance. Do
              you not think carefully of where

you sit? Today as the servers stream
              in and out, you will
be a shocking sight. The plastic-strip
              door will flap, beat with the
back of hands. Rattling hands will fist
              at where you sit. The thin paint
of the wall will protest and flake

          on your shoulders. I will look

at you longer than anyone else
              eating alone at longer tables.
The hard-backed chairs will wobble
              in anger. Listen to the preponderant,

faux pas are inexcusable.

We Buried Her in Compost

When I brushed my mother's hair for the first time, the comb
buckled and broke. Her hair choked the bristles in fits
of courage—I saw the martyred soldiers resisting the free

fall, I saw their gentle bodies resting on the yarn, I saw
them sinking to the bottom of the maroon carpet, I saw
them darkening the borders of dirt-smudged flowers.

We laid it to rest on her birthday. Forty-three candles lit
on wooden stands dripped skin and bones onto my mother's
martyrs. Theatres of war change from year to year, as do

front room carpets. We make a tradition of it, of tapestry
baked into compost lasagne. Look carefully before
the year is up—my worms eat her flowers, her stems pull

and twist and break, her leaves thread out in kitchen waste.
If I were an artist, I told my mother, I'd sew onion peels
and carrot tops. Flowers are scent and beauty and show,

but I need garbage for my carpet gateau.

Summers With You

Today the crack and arch of ice trays gives me
sweet, sugar-tumbles of salted-apple cubes
browned in the sun
browned by the pink of salt.
Sweet summer is sour lemons, squeezed
into thick mugs at organic stores I see

only with you—reading labels out
like school morning recitations, stop
with the definitions
when you don't know. Every day you
question and I red-heart queries and other
unsubstantiated points in blue textbooks.
My highlights will fade with future
infras.
Listen—do you hear the soft erasure of your pencil marks
while you play
    Pictionary
        under your
            pupils
In the light of the night?

Prelude to 'This Is Just to Say'*

Standing by the
plum tree you
picked the
reddest,
ripest,
prettiest fruits.

I saw a
circus fade.

On a new day
seasons hence,
we will have
fresher plums—

but
I'll still
remember
the flesh
of the pits
carved in.

---

*Williams, William Carlos, 'This Is Just To Say,' in *The Collected Poems: Volume I*, 1909-1939, edited by Litz, A. Walton and MacGowan, Christopher, New Directions Publishing Corporation, 1991.

Painting Skin on Skin

I am a complex subject. I imagine it will be harder to paint
my colours,
ones you won't find in 24 sets—
they have to be constructed. Only the true artist can
scale my peaks and slide down my valleys.

My ripples are pink at epicentre and brown into
the grass as they move ahead. You cannot monochrome
me, your pastels will sieve through the canvas and to the
floor like they never were.

Only my colours stick to sheets, so when you paint me,
paint me carefully.

Bhavyakirti

Full Moons

What do full moons do?
Over the month they go around and chew everyone out.
Skeletons are skewers, once a month they gloat and
 regurgitate.

What do full moons do?
They measure distance. T months from when we oiled our
hands on thin bread. Today, you sit in front of your screens—
O, one of the mendicant orders.

What do I do to full moons?
Mostly I avoid, blanketed in brick. If I look, it's with the
beating heart of the bass in my ears. The rattle of
gyrus and skull, and the moon's
dimples clear out.

What is this?
Perfection, and reverie.

In Memoriam

I.

A cacophony of sounds;
that is what war sounds like.

It is the squelch of flesh
on flesh on fresh
wounds,
the familiar click in
the hands of soldiers
muted to their consciences
with the frequency of a
dripping tap that is
lived with, for years,
but not fixed.

II.

Focus.
Scientists have developed
deep ridges of
seriousness and worry
appears on their precious
foreheads, so much so, it
resembles the matter
inside.

III.

M&M.
Machine to man.
Machine to man
as wizards spell over
blocks of iron
and rubber veins,
lifetimes fly and a
question remains on the
corner of the page on
which they made notes.

How to make a machine,
a man?
Red, circled twice and
underlined.

IV.

Reverse.
Two little triangles that
point to the left
The problem became
a little simpler
now again it is read
in rooms with
more important people,

how to make a man
a machine?

A gun-toting fellow
is told a few words
through mouths
that work magic.

V.

Great,
is what they'll be called
for this
because, glory?
That
comes packed and
sealed in cocked guns
and hand grenades,
more of it as the
size increases
of course.

VI.

Reverse.
Two little triangles that
point to the left
because to not be
right is to go left,
that is, backwards,

but who decided that
the right is right?
For my right may not be yours.

VII.

Two persons
stand facing
each other, gazing
into the eyes of a
stranger they'd never
met before.

They think not;
for to differ must mean
that the piece is
defective.

But to do as told,
wears it down until
the wires inside fuse
together and can
never be fixed.

I Stopped Seeing People Again Today*

Aren't **all** mind readers;
Guess have to accept that;
that can't get into everyone's mind;
can't accept;
will slowly shovel into head;
won't drill;
will match rhythm of heart;
So never know what happened.
will sit with brain mass;
won't know what to do with;
will double tweeze neurons from one another;
create bigger synapses;
help nobody;
get confused.

---

*Part of a short story titled 'I Stopped Seeing People Again Today' published on my Medium page.

Rails Are Midnight to Me

I.

At 5 she is awake.
The passing rail trembles as she
picks up her jug of water to
save from spills of overcrowding.

II.

Her saree tapers at
its waisted knot
pulled distant from sequined
dust pans lying creviced
in webs of thread
lint balled on knees
never reveals the
soft abrasions within
days are festive
so festive is the cloth.

III.

Rails are midnight to me
soft jingles of industrial dance
a salt shaker rotates, stills
flat pivots and nights go on.

Empty Hand Cream

My empty bottle of hand cream
rests its head upon the bin, like lovers
nestled under a tree in a book read.

Not within, just outside, someone's
missed aim, a mock, a jest,
conversational quips, a love story.

The nozzle sighs in deep resignation,
of rattle and the fall of loose knobs,
the terror of hand-pulling by a

gust of wind, or phantom football
kicks, or responsible citizens
emptying trash.

Seating Them on Park Benches

Occupied nodal benches seat them—
resting their elbows on plaid
wrapped femurs.

Tires swing in pendulum,
as do faces seating unspectacled eyes
spotting insects trawled in wind.

Unspectacled eyes
soft edges
airbrush crawling brown toddlers
in the mud.

Nubivagant motions raise
leisurely arms,
creak
cement
benches,
like planked floors.

Bouquets of hands obscure in suited flâneur pockets.
Bouquets of hands that I cannot count.
Bouquets of pockets hiding hands like the last supper.

Mumbai

I had refused to believe the water
was glittery until I saw it for myself.
It folded and unfolded—creases of moss
ripping suddenly parallel to the sadness
of bush and tree.

Birth

Bazaars make them
the poet, the artist,
the shy girl listening to the
whir of the roasting machines,
the children that look at glass
and retreat imagining its shatter,
the children that look though glass
at wet cake, splat on a quarter-plate
before a laptop.
Something brews there—
(a narrative on yellow sheets stained
with oily fingers at turns)
coffee.

Quantum

Quantum of death? No. Quantum.
Who did you lose? One lakh a month.
I lost 70,000. Ok. You can
weep ahead.

Each and every person within these
walls, weighs heavy with the grief
of a billion. Better to weep about
smaller sums.

What Will You Do?

What will you do if your name is called only in
the monotone of a rail announcer? Angled glances
at dinner tables keep you up at night. What if those
who named you grow up to detest you? Maturity

isn't exclusive to tighter skins. What will you do when
luck runs out? The spots bounce off your die and
waddle unto the front lawn. They might metamorphize
faster than you can run and crawl up to the tree tops.

Will you hang them from the clips attached to the
empty clothes line? (Careful! Lest you burn your
palms brushing past the cord) Will you let them
dance in the wind by your lucky tie?

What will you do when the Listerine dries out
your bones? Your blue teeth tempt old jewellers.
Sapphire enamels and purpled gum—and suddenly
everyone wants to hear you speak. When will you

tell them you are mute?

Fish Tank

Then my mother
pooled me in her
hands like

hollow marbles—
the ecstasy of
a child cupping

their palms in
a puddle, pulling
tadpoles out. She

keeps me in a thin
low walled fish
tank. When her

weeds get my
fingers, I weep
and wave my

flippers. She snips
the greens and
clears the tank

of my dirt.

Summer Love

Summer love is watching your mother run
a blunting knife through the flesh of fruit.
You emote not at the dripping syrup, but
at fingers softening cold white pits.
You could be gut today, your senses
Shelled, deseeded—
(Am I a low hanging fruit?)
but you won't recall your own
scent as you pulp. You'll remember the
stick of the mango, the slow pry of your
sugar-glazed forearms tearing away
from the kitchen slab, the wet slap of a
porous cloth on yellowed marble, the
quick dry of moisture lasered by the
rusted exhaust.

You'll remember looking at her dimpled
cheeks and never complaining of craters in
pear again. She'll remember looking at
the dawdle of a baby red-wattled lapwing
learning to fly

from the kitchen window
as she slices away peels.

Qualifications I Don't Have to Write My First Book

Should I qualify in Creative Writing?
Because that's what other creative writers do.
I slap the butter of words across stale bread,
but serve it warm and toasty to you.

I pen rhymes, and some are fine,
but some would be plain poor in view.
In those that I have thrown away,
the ones I regret are few.

Yet, in all my friends now and the ones before,
the ones who have met my parents too,
no one would know me better
than you, here, finishing my debut.